# The Reluctant Dragon

PERFORMANCE EDITION

Adapted from *"The Reluctant Dragon"* by Kenneth Grahame.

by Querida Funck

Published by Lemery House Press

# Copyright

The Reluctant Dragon: Performance Edition
Adapted from "The Reluctant Dragon" by Kenneth Grahame
Copyright © Querida Funck 2025
Published by Lemery House Press

All rights reserved. No part of this adaptation or abridged edition may be reproduced, stored in a retrieval system, or transmitted in any form or by any means—electronic, mechanical, photocopying, recording, or otherwise—without the prior written permission of the publisher, except in the case of brief quotations used in reviews or scholarly works.

This is a work of creative adaptation or abridgment. While based on a public domain original, the structure, editorial arrangement, and any additional commentary or thematic framing are original contributions by the adapter and are protected by copyright.

## Other Performance Editions
### *for Actors, Educators, and Storytellers*

**A Room And A Voice**
(based on work by Virginia Woolf)
**The White Heron**
(based on the work of Sarah Orne Jewett)
**The Light Princess**
(based on the work of George MacDonald)
**Miss Grief**
(based on the work of Constance Fenimore Woolson)

☙

### Coming in 2025

**Life As It Is (More or Less)**
(based on the work of Fanny Fern)
**The Selfish Giant**
(based on the work of Oscar Wilde)
**Thanksgiving Time**
(based on the work of Laura Ingalls Wilder – originally credited to A. J. Wilder)
**The Happy Prince**
(based on the work of Oscar Wilde)
**The Forsaken Merman**
(based on the work of Matthew Arnold)

# Dedication

For those who still believe that wonder is not just for children—
who hear truth tucked inside a jest,
who smile at dragons that write poetry,
and who know that every fable hides a lesson worth carrying forward.

# Foreword

This title is part of the Modern Fables for Grown-Ups theme—tales with a twist, a truth, or a touch of magic. These editions combine timeless literature with fresh insights from an actor's and narrator's perspective, offering both the pleasure of the story and the craft of telling it well. In audio, this piece runs approximately thirty minutes, making it ideal for thoughtful listening in a single sitting. Intentional Listening Rating: PG – Thoughtful Themes.

In about thirty minutes, *The Reluctant Dragon* delivers a complete arc you can program anywhere—classrooms, book clubs, libraries, salons, or small theatres—while still leaving time for Q&A or a companion piece. It's a compact study of recognition and the cost of being heard, ideal for practicing subtle performance and inviting audiences to wrestle with who gets called "genius" (and who doesn't).

**Kenneth Grahame (1859–1932)** was a Scottish writer best known for his classic children's books. His work blends gentle humor, myth, and pastoral storytelling, offering timeless reflections on friendship, courage, and imagination.

> "The whole book breathes of that sense of 'otherness' which clings to all childhood, of mystery and wonder, of adventure and romance, of the beauty and the strangeness of things."
>
> — Kenneth Grahame, *Dream Days* (1898)

# About The Series

True Voice Shorts is a curated collection of enhanced audio and literary editions that reimagine classic works, personal essays, modern fables, and original tales. Some stories are adapted or abridged with care—preserving the heart of the original while offering clarity and accessibility for contemporary audiences. Others are new, crafted to speak with honesty, nuance, and emotional depth.

This series was created for thoughtful readers and listeners who seek stories that linger—brief in form, but rich in meaning. Whether drawn from forgotten voices of the past or imagined anew, each piece offers a quiet invitation to pause, reflect, and connect.

The **Performance Editions** extend this mission by pairing the literary work with insights from the stage and the recording booth—guidance on historical and literary context, analysis of story and character arcs, and practical techniques for bringing the piece to life through reading or performance. Designed for actors, voice artists, educators, and literature lovers, these editions celebrate not only the story on the page, but the art of telling it aloud.

From whispered memory to gentle magic, from resilience to rediscovered identity, these stories are short by design—but lasting in resonance.

You may choose to read the story straight through for enjoyment, or explore the performance notes and storytelling guides before or after reading to deepen your understanding and delivery.

## About the Authors

**Querida Funck** is an author/playwright, stage director, voice artist, and the founder of Lemery House Press. She crafts adaptations that honor the rhythm of language and the intimacy of voice, blending old truths with new perspectives. Her work explores memory, identity, and transformation—often in quiet, poetic ways. As a stage director, she brings a deep understanding of pacing, movement, and visual storytelling, skills that inform both her performance work and her editorial approach.

As the creator of the True Voice Shorts series, she brings short fiction and forgotten classics to life in both audio and print, celebrating the enduring power of story across generations.

For more about the Modern Fables for Grown-Ups series, visit Lemery House Press online

☙

**Kenneth Grahame (1859–1932)** was a Scottish-born writer whose imaginative works continue to enchant readers more than a century after their publication. Best remembered for *The Wind in the Willows* (1908) and the earlier tale *The Reluctant Dragon* (1898), Grahame's writing blends gentle humor, myth, and pastoral storytelling, offering timeless reflections on friendship, courage, and the transformative power of imagination.

Born in Edinburgh, Grahame lost his mother at the age of five, a tragedy that marked his early childhood. His father, unable to cope, sent Kenneth and his siblings to live with their grandmother in the Berkshire countryside. This move profoundly shaped his inner world: the meadows, streams, and lanes around Cookham Dean would later inspire the landscapes of *The Wind in the Willows*, where the natural world is rendered with reverence both idyllic and deeply personal.

Denied the opportunity to attend Oxford due to financial constraints, Grahame instead entered the Bank of England, where he rose to the position of Secretary. Though he achieved professional success, his true passion remained storytelling. He began publishing essays and sketches in the 1880s, collected in volumes such as *Pagan Papers* (1893) and *The Golden Age* (1895). These works nostalgically recall the secret kingdoms of childhood, written with a wistful tone that balances playfulness with an undercurrent of melancholy.

It was in *Dream Days* (1898), a sequel to *The Golden Age*, where *The Reluctant Dragon* first appeared. This witty inversion of the traditional dragon-slaying tale introduces a peaceable, poetry-loving dragon and a sensible boy who questions the need for violence. The story satirizes convention and celebrates imagination over brute force, themes that would resonate even more strongly in Grahame's later work.

Grahame's personal life was often marked by difficulty. His marriage to Elspeth Thomson was strained, and their only child, Alastair—nicknamed "Mouse"—struggled with health issues and depression. Grahame's bedtime stories for Alastair, featuring Mole, Rat, Toad, and Badger, became the foundation of *The Wind in the Willows.* Published in 1908, the novel was initially met with mixed reviews, but it soon grew into a beloved classic, praised for its lyrical depictions of the English countryside and its endearing characters.

In his later years, Grahame retired to the countryside, where he lived quietly, removed from public life. He never wrote another major book, but his reputation only grew after his death in 1932. Today, his works remain cornerstones of children's literature, treasured by both young readers and adults who find in them a reflection of innocence, friendship, and the longing for a world where kindness and imagination prevail.

Kenneth Grahame's legacy is one of quiet revolution. By imbuing his stories with warmth, irony, and a refusal to accept violence as inevitable, he created fables that continue to charm and challenge us—reminders that sometimes the bravest heroes are those who choose peace over battle, and that even dragons may prefer poetry to war.

# Guide to Effective Storytelling

## Historical & Literary Context

Kenneth Grahame wrote *The Reluctant Dragon* at the close of the Victorian era, first publishing it in *Dream Days* (1898). At that time, Britain was steeped in heroic and imperial ideals—stories of knights, conquest, and noble combat were common in both children's literature and popular culture. Yet Grahame's fable gently subverts these expectations.

Instead of glorifying battle, he imagines a dragon who is peaceable, indolent, and literary, preferring poetry to pillaging. The Boy is not a damsel in distress but a calm, rational mediator, while St. George is less a fearsome warrior than a pragmatic gentleman willing to bend tradition. This humorous reversal reflected Grahame's larger literary project: to honor the imagination and perspective of children while quietly questioning adult seriousness, duty, and violence.

Within its cultural moment, *The Reluctant Dragon* was both familiar—borrowing the trappings of legend—and radical, presenting a world where conflict can be staged rather than real, and where kindness triumphs over fear.

## Story Arc & Character Arc

Although light in tone, the story follows a clear dramatic structure that performers can use as a guide:

- **Exposition:** The Shepherd discovers the Dragon and is terrified. The Boy is introduced as calm and bookish, unafraid of what others dread.
- **Rising Action:** The Boy meets the Dragon, who confesses his laziness and love of poetry. Their conversations reveal that he is no monster at all.

- **Conflict:** The villagers demand the Dragon be slain. St. George arrives, embodying tradition and expectation. The Boy mediates between hero and dragon.
- **Climax:** A staged "battle" satisfies appearances, allowing both sides to maintain dignity without violence.
- **Resolution:** Harmony is restored. The Dragon remains free, the villagers are content, and the Boy's wisdom is vindicated.

**Character arcs:**

- **The Boy:** Begins as a curious child, becomes the story's true mediator and voice of reason.
- **The Dragon:** Shifts from isolated and indolent to socially engaged, even if still reluctant to change.
- **St. George:** Moves from rigid duty to pragmatic compromise, showing flexibility within tradition.

  **The Villagers** remain fearful but are pacified by appearances — a reminder that spectacle often matters more to society than substance.

## Actor/Voice Actor Techniques for Storytelling

Performing *The Reluctant Dragon* benefits from tonal variety and contrasts. Each character carries a distinct rhythm, allowing even a solo performer to create differentiation without caricature.

- **The Shepherd:** Nervous, hesitant, prone to agitation. Use a tremor in pacing or a breathy delivery to capture his fear.
- **The Boy:** Grounded, thoughtful, quietly amused. A steady, even tone conveys his wisdom, while hints of humor underline his role as the voice of reason.
- **The Dragon:** Lazy, witty, endearing or perhaps even dramatic. Speak with unhurried rhythm, elongated vowels, and playful warmth. Occasional bashfulness when discussing poetry contrasts with his otherwise languid charm.

- **St. George:** Noble, courteous, and formal. A clear, resonant tone—slightly declamatory—underscores his knightly bearing. Later, soften the voice to show his willingness to compromise.
- **The Villagers:** Collective energy, excitable and fearful. A brisk, murmuring delivery or overlapping "chorus" of voices (if ensemble) conveys their restless anxiety.

**Narration:** Should be lively and lightly ironic, inviting the audience to share in the humor. Use pacing to highlight reversals: a pause before "It's only a dragon" lets the line land with comic weight.

Performers should embrace the irony and warmth at the heart of the story. The humor lies not in exaggeration, but in understatement: the Dragon's reluctance to fight, the Boy's matter-of-fact calm, and the gentle absurdity of a staged battle. Delivered with charm, these contrasts allow the story's themes—peace over violence, imagination over fear—to resonate clearly.

## Effective Staging & Embodied Storytelling

While *The Reluctant Dragon* is delightful as a read-aloud or audio performance, it also lends itself to simple staging. Whether presented by a single storyteller or a small cast, the tale's humor and irony come alive when embodied.

**For a solo performer:**

- Use **shifts in stance and posture** to signal character changes. For example, the Shepherd might hunch anxiously, while the Dragon reclines with lazy ease.
- **Voice placement** can distinguish roles without elaborate acting—lighter and curious for the Boy, deep and unhurried for the Dragon, formal and ringing for St. George.
- Minimal props (a book, a cloak, a staff) can serve multiple symbolic functions, keeping the focus on the words.

**For a small cast:**

- Two to three performers can divide narration and roles, allowing for playful interaction. One might serve as primary narrator, while the others embody characters in dialogue.
- Scenes such as the Boy meeting the Dragon or the villagers greeting St. George can be staged with **simple blocking**, using levels and distance to show relationship and tension.
- Because the story pivots on contrast—fear vs. calm, violence vs. poetry—actors can lean into **physical opposites**: nervous fidgeting beside serene stillness, rigid formality against relaxed sprawl.

**For both solo and ensemble versions:**

- Emphasize **theatrical storytelling rather than realism**. A bare stage, a chair, or even a reading stand is enough; the performer's voice and presence create the imaginative space.
- Pauses are as important as dialogue. A held silence after "It's only a dragon" or before the reluctant "battle" can let the humor land with the audience.
- End with warmth: the Dragon's poetry, St. George's gentleness, and the Boy's calm common sense invite a reflective close rather than a triumphant finale.

By treating the piece as **story-theatre**, performers highlight its wit and fable-like qualities. In doing so, the audience is reminded that the power of a tale does not rest on spectacle, but on the storyteller's ability to invite listeners into a shared act of imagination.

**Audience Engagement**

Stories live not only in words, but in the relationship between teller and listener. *The Reluctant Dragon* offers unique opportunities to adapt tone, pacing, and style depending on the audience.

**For adults (Modern Fables for Grown-Ups):**

- Lean into irony and satire—highlight the humor in villagers' fear and the absurdity of tradition.
- Use pauses to let witty reversals land, inviting reflective smiles.
- Emphasize the philosophical undertone: imagination and poetry can be stronger than violence.

**For children or mixed-age audiences:**

- Bring out the Dragon's humor and warmth with playful delivery.
- Keep pacing lively, especially in scenes of the villagers' chatter or the Dragon's bashful poetry.
- Encourage laughter and interaction—audiences relish the tension between the Boy's calmness and the adults' panic.

**For classrooms or group storytelling:**

- Encourage participation: ask what they think the Dragon should do, or how the "battle" might end.
- Use simple gestures or minimal staging to spark imagination without needing props.

No matter what the audience, the heart of the story lies in **connection**: drawing listeners into a shared recognition that tradition can be questioned, and that gentleness can be heroic.

# The Reluctant Dragon

*The following text is adapted from Kenneth Grahame's 1898 story as it appeared in Dream Days.*

Long ago, there might have been hundreds of years ago—in a cottage half-way between this village and yonder shoulder of the Downs up there, a shepherd lived with his wife and their little son. Now the shepherd spent his days—and at certain times of the year his nights too—up on the wide ocean-bosom of the Downs, with only the sun and the stars and the sheep for company, and the friendly chattering world of men and women far out of sight arid hearing.

But his little son, when he wasn't helping his father, and often when he was as well, spent much of his time buried in big volumes that he borrowed from the affable gentry and interested persons of the country round about. And his parents were very fond of him, and rather proud of him too, though they didn't let on in his hearing, so he was left to go his own way and read as much as he liked; and instead of frequently getting a cuff on the side of the head, as might very well have happened to him, he was treated more or less as an equal by his parents, who sensibly thought it a very fair division of labor that they should supply the practical knowledge, and he the book-learning.

They knew that book-learning often came in useful at a pinch, in spite of what their neighbors said.

What the Boy chiefly dabbled in was natural history and fairy tales, and he just took them as they came, in a sandwichy sort of way, without making any distinctions; and really his course of reading strikes one as rather sensible.

One evening the shepherd, who for some nights past had been disturbed and preoccupied, and off his usual mental balance, came home all of a tremble, and, sitting down at the table where his wife and son were peacefully employed, she with her seam, he in following out the adventures of the Giant with no Heart in his Body, exclaimed with much agitation:

"It's all up to me, Maria! Never no more can I go up on them there Downs, was it ever so!"

"Now don't you take on like that," said his wife, who was a very sensible woman: "but tell us all about it first, whatever it is as has given you this shake-up, and then me and you and the son here, between us, we ought to be able to get to the bottom of it!"

"It began some nights ago," said the shepherd. "You know that cave up there—I never liked it, somehow, and the sheep never liked it neither, and when sheep don't like a thing there's generally some reason for it. Well, for some time past there's been faint noises coming from that cave—noises like heavy sightings, with grunts mixed up in them; and sometimes snoring, far away down-real snoring, yet somehow not honest snoring, like you and me o'nights, you know!"

"I know," remarked the Boy, quietly.

"Of course I was terrible frightened," the shepherd went on; "yet somehow I couldn't keep away. So this very evening, before I come down, I took a cast round by the cave, quietly. And there— O Lord! there I saw him at last, as plain as I see you!"

"Saw who?" said his wife, beginning to share in her husband's nervous terror.

"Why him, I'm a telling you!" said the shepherd. "He was sticking half-way out of the cave, and seemed to be enjoying of the cool of the evening in a poetical sort of way. He was as big as four carthorses, and all covered with shiny scales—deep-blue scales at the top of him, shading off to a tender sort of' green below. As he breathed, there was that sort of flicker over his nostrils that you see over our chalk roads on a baking windless day in summer. He had his chin on his paws, and I should say he was meditating about things.

Oh, yes, a peaceable sort of o' beast enough, and not ramping or carrying on or doing anything but what was quite right and proper. I admit all that. And yet, what am I to do? Scales, you know, and claws, and a tail for certain, though I didn't see that end of him—I ain't used to 'em, and I don't hold with 'em, and That's a fact!"

The Boy, who had been absorbed in his book during his father's recital, now closed the volume, yawned, clasped his hands behind his head, and said sleepily:
"It's all right, father. Don't you worry. It's only a dragon."

"Only a dragon?" cried his father. "What do you mean, sitting there, you and your dragons? Only a dragon indeed! And what do you know about it?"

'cos it is, and cos I do know," replied the Boy, quietly. "Look here, father, you know we've each of us got our line. You know about sheep, and weather, and things; I know about dragons. I always said, you know, that that cave up there was a dragon-cave. I always said it must have belonged to a dragon for some time, and ought to belong to a dragon now, if rules count for anything. Well, now you tell me it has a dragon, and so That's all right. I'm not half as surprised as you told me it hadn't got a dragon. Rules always come right if you wait quietly."

"Now, please, just leave this all to me. And I'll stroll up to-morrow morning—no, in the morning I can't, I've got a whole heap of things to do—well, in the evening, if I'm quite free, I'll go up and have a talk to him, and you'll find it'll be all right. Only, please, don't you go worrying round there without me. You don't understand 'em a bit, and they're very sensitive, you know!"

"He's quite right, father," said the sensible mother. "As he says, dragons is his line and not ours. He's wonderful knowing about book beasts, as everyone allows. And to tell the truth, I'm not half happy in my own mind, thinking of that poor animal lying alone up there, without a bit o" hot supper or anyone to change the news with; and maybe we'll be able to do something for him; and if he ain't quite respectable our Boy will find it out quick enough. He's got a pleasant sort of way with him that makes everybody tell him everything.

Next day, after he'd had his tea, the Boy strolled up the chalky track that led to the summit of the Downs; and there, sure enough, he found the dragon, stretched lazily on the sward in front of his cave. The view from that point was a magnificent one. To the right and left, the bare and willowy leagues of Downs; in front, the vale, with its clustered homesteads, its threads of white roads running through orchards and well- tilled acreage, and, far away, a hint of old grey cities on the horizon. A cool breeze played over the surface of the grass and the silver shoulder of a large moon was showing above distant junipers.

No wonder the dragon seemed in a peaceful and contented mood; indeed, as the Boy approached he could hear the beast purring with a happy regularity. "Well, we live and learn!" he said to himself.

"None of my books ever told me that dragons purred!"

"Hullo, dragon!" said the Boy, quietly, when he had gotten up to him.

The dragon, on hearing the approaching footsteps, made the beginning of a courteous effort to rise. But when he saw it was a Boy, he set his eyebrows severely.

"Now don't you hit me," he said; "or bung stones, or squirt water, or anything. I won't have it, I tell you!"

"Not going' to hit you," said the Boy, wearily, dropping on the grass beside the beast: "and don't, for goodness" sake, keep on saying "Don't"; I hear so much of it, and It's monotonous, and makes me tired. I've simply looked in to ask you how you were and all that sort of thing; but if I'm in the way I can easily clear out. I've lots of friends, and no one can say I'm in the habit of shoving myself in where I'm not wanted!"

"No, no, don't go off in a huff," said the dragon, hastily; "fact is,—I'm as happy up here as the day's long; never without an occupation, dear fellow, never without an occupation! And yet, between ourselves, it is a trifle dull at times."

The Boy bit off a stalk of grass and chewed it. "Going to make a long stay here?" he asked, politely.

"Can't hardly say at present," replied the dragon. "It seems a nice place enough—but I've only been here a short time, and one must look about and reflect and consider before settling down. It's rather a serious thing, settling down. Besides—now I'm going to tell you something! You'd never guess it if you tried ever so!—fact is I'm such a confoundedly lazy beggar!"

"You surprise me," said the Boy, civilly.

"It's the sad truth," the dragon went on, settling down between his paws and evidently delighted to have found a listener at last: "and I fancy That's really how I came to be here. You see all the other fellows were so active and earnest and all that sort of thing—always rampaging, and skirmishing, and scouring the desert sands, and pacing the margin of the sea, and chasing knights all over the place, and devouring damsels, and going on generally—whereas I liked to get my meals regular and then to prop my back against a bit of rock and snooze a bit, and wake up and think of things going on and how they kept going on just the same, you know! So when it happened I got fairly caught."

"When what happened, please?" asked the Boy.

"That's just what I don't precisely know," said the dragon. "I suppose the earth sneezed, or shook itself, or the bottom dropped out of something. Anyhow there was a shake and a roar and a general stramash, and I found myself miles away underground and wedged in as tight as tight."

" Well, thank goodness, my wants are few, and at any rate I had peace and quietness and wasn't always being asked to come along and do something. And I've got such an active mind—always occupied, I assure you! But time went on, and there was a certain sameness about the life, and at last I began to think it would be fun to work my way upstairs and see what you other fellows were doing. So I scratched and burrowed, and worked this way and that way and at last I came out through this cave here. And I like the country, and the view, and the people—what I've seen of 'em—and on the whole I feel inclined to settle down here."

"What's your mind always occupied about?" asked the Boy. "That's what I want to know."

The dragon colored slightly and looked away. Presently he said bashfully: "Did you ever—just for fun—try to make up poetry—verses, you know?"

"Course I have," said the Boy. "Heaps of it. And some of It's quite good, I feel sure, only there's no one here cares about it. Mother's very kind and all that, when I read it to her, and so's father for that matter. But somehow they don't seem to—"

"Exactly," cried the dragon; "my own case exactly. They don't seem to, and you can't argue with 'em about it. Now you've got culture, you have, I could tell it on you at once, and I should just like your candid opinion about some little things I threw off lightly, when I was down there. I'm awfully pleased to have met you, and I'm hoping the other neighbors will be equally agreeable. There was a very nice old gentleman up here only last night, but he didn't seem to want to intrude."

"That was my father," said the Boy, "and he is a nice old gentleman, and I'll introduce you some day if you like."

"Can't you two come up here and dine or something to-morrow?" asked the dragon, eagerly. "Only, of course, if you've got nothing better to do," he added politely.

"Thanks awfully," said the Boy, "but we don't go out anywhere without my mother, and, to tell you the truth, I'm afraid she mightn't quite approve of you. You see there's no getting over the hard fact that you're a dragon, is there? And when you talk of settling down, and the neighbors, and so on, I can't help feeling that you don't quite realize your position. You're an enemy of the human race, you see!"

"Haven't got an enemy in the world," said the dragon, cheerfully. "Too lazy to make 'em, to begin with. And if I do read other fellows my poetry, I'm always ready to listen to theirs!"

"Oh, dear!" cried the Boy, "I wish You'd try and grasp the situation properly. When the other people find you out, they'll come after you with spears and swords and all sorts of things. You'll have to be exterminated, according to their way of looking at it! You're a scourge, and a pest, and a baneful monster!"

"Not a word of truth in it," said the dragon, wagging his head solemnly. "Character will bear the strictest investigation. And now, there's a little sonnet-thing I was working on when you appeared on the scene—"

"Oh, if you won't be sensible: cried the Boy, getting up, "I'm going off home. No, I can't stop for sonnets; my mother's sitting up. I'll look you up to-morrow, sometime or other, and do for goodness" sake try and realize that You're a pestilential scourge, or you'll find yourself in a most awful fix. Good night!"

The Boy found it an easy matter to set the mind of his parents at ease about his new friend. They had always left that branch to him, and they took his word without a murmur. The shepherd was formally introduced and many compliments and kind inquiries were exchanged. His wife, however, though expressing her willingness to do anything she could,—to mend things, or set the cave to rights, or cook a little something when the dragon had been poring over sonnets and forgotten his meals, as male things will do,—could not be brought to recognize him formally.

The fact that he was a dragon and "they didn't know who he was" seemed to count for everything with her. She made no objection, however, to her little son spending his evenings with the dragon quietly, so long as he was home by nine o'clock: and many a pleasant night they had, sitting on the sward, while the dragon told stories of old, old times, when dragons were quite plentiful and the world was a livelier place than it is now, and life was full of thrills and jumps and surprises.

What the Boy had feared, however, soon came to pass. The most modest and retiring dragon in the world, if He's as big as four carthorses and covered with blue scales, cannot keep altogether out of the public view.

And so in the village tavern of nights the fact that a real live dragon sat brooding in the cave on the Downs was naturally a subject for talk.

Though the villagers were extremely frightened, they were rather proud as well. It was a distinction to have a dragon of your own, and it was felt to be a feather in the cap of the village. Still, all we're agreed that this sort of thing couldn't be allowed to go on. The dreadful beast must be exterminated, the countryside must be freed from this pest, this terror, this destroying scourge. The fact that not even a hen-roost was the worst because the dragon's arrival wasn't allowed to have anything to do with it. He was a dragon, and he couldn't deny it, and if he didn't choose to behave as such that was his own lookout.

But in spite of much valiant talk no hero was found willing to take sword and spear and free the suffering village and win deathless fame; and each night's heated discussion always ended in nothing. Meanwhile the dragon, a happy Bohemian, lolled on the turf, enjoyed the sunsets, told antediluvian anecdotes to the Boy, and polished his old verses while meditating on fresh ones.

One day the Boy, on walking into the village, found everything wearing a festal appearance which was not to be accounted for in the calendar. Carpets and gay-colored stuffs were hung out of the windows, the church-bells clamored noisily, the little street was flower-strewn, and the whole population jostled each other along either side of it, chattering, shoving, and ordering each other to stand back.

The Boy saw a friend of his own age in the crowd and hailed him.

"What's up?" he cried. "Is it the players, or bears, or a circus, or what?"
"It's all right," his friend hailed back. "He's a coming."

"Who's a-coming?" demanded the Boy, thrusting into the throng.

"Why, St George, of course," replied his friend. "He's heard tell of our dragon, and He's coming on purpose to slay the deadly beast, and free us from his horrid yoke. Oh my! won't there be a jolly fight!"

Here was news indeed! The Boy felt that he ought to make quite sure for himself, and he wriggled himself in between the legs of his good-natured elders, abusing them all the time for their unmannerly habit of shoving. Once in the front rank, he breathlessly awaited the arrival.

Presently from the far-away end of the line came the sound of cheering. Next, the measured tramp of a great war-horse made his heartbeat quicker, and then he found himself cheering with the rest, as, amidst welcoming shouts, shrill cries of women, uplifting of babies and waving of handkerchiefs, St George paced slowly up the street. The Boy's heart stood still and he breathed with sobs, the beauty and the grace of the hero were so far beyond anything he had yet seen. His fluted armor was inlaid with gold, his plumed helmet hung at his saddlebow, and his thick fair hair framed a face gracious and gentle beyond expression till you caught the sternness in his eyes.

He drew rein in front of the little inn, and the villagers crowded round with greetings and thanks and voluble statements of their wrongs and grievances and oppressions. The Boy heard the grave gentle voice of the Saint, assuring them that all would be well now, and that he would stand by them and see them righted and free them from their foe; then he dismounted and passed through the doorway and the crowd poured in after him. But the Boy made off up the hill as fast as he could lay his legs to the ground.

"It's all up, dragon!" he shouted as soon as he was within sight of the beast. "He's coming! He's here now! You'll have to pull yourself together and do something at last!" The dragon was licking his scales and rubbing them with a bit of house-flannel the Boy's mother had lent him, till he shone like a great turquoise.

"Don't be violent, Boy," he said without looking round. "Sit down and get your breath, and try and remember that the noun governs the verb, and then perhaps you'll be good enough to tell me who's coming?"

"That's right, take it coolly," said the Boy. "Hope you'll be half as cool when I've got through with my news. It's only St George who's coming, That's all; he rode into the village half-an-hour ago. Of course you can lick him—a great big fellow like you! But I thought I'd warn you, 'cos He's sure to be round early, and He's got the longest, wickedest-looking spear you ever did see!" And the boy got up and began to jump round in sheer delight at the prospect of the battle.

"0 deary, deary me," moaned the dragon; "this is too awful. I won't see him, and That's flat. I don't want to know the fellow at all. I'm sure He's not nice. You must tell him to go away at once, please. Say he can write if he likes, but I can't give him an interview. I'm not seeing anybody at present."

"Now dragon, dragon;" said the Boy, imploringly, "don't be perverse and wrongheaded. You've got to fight him some time or other, you know, 'cos He's St George and You're the dragon. Better get it over, and then we can go on with the sonnets. And you ought to consider other people a little, too. If It's been dull up here for you, think how dull It's been for me!"

"My dear little man," said the dragon, solemnly, "just understand, once for all, that I can't fight and I won't fight. I've never fought in my life, and I'm not going to begin now, just to give you a Roman holiday. In old days I always let the other fellows—the earnest fellows—do all the fighting, and no doubt That's why I have the pleasure of being here now."

"But if you don't fight he'll cut your head off!" gasped the Boy, miserable at the prospect of losing both his fight and his friend.

"Oh, I think not," said the dragon in his lazy way. "You'll be able to arrange something. I've every confidence in you, You're such a manager. Just run down, there's a dear chap, and make it all right. I leave it entirely to you."

The Boy made his way back to the village in a state of great despondency. First of all, there wasn't going to be any fight; next, his dear and honored friend the dragon hadn't shown up in quite such a heroic light as he would have liked; and lastly, whether the dragon was a hero at heart or not, it made no difference, for St George would most undoubtedly cut his head off. "Arrange things indeed!" he said bitterly to himself. "The dragon treats the whole affair as if it was an invitation to tea and croquet."

The villagers were straggling homewards as he passed up the street, all of them in the highest spirits, and gleefully discussing the splendid fight that was in store. The Boy pursued his way to the inn, and passed into the principal chamber, where St George now sat alone, musing over the chances of the fight, and the sad stories of rapine and of wrong that had so lately been poured into his sympathetic ears.

"May I come in, St George?" said the Boy, politely, as he paused at the door. "I want to talk to you about this little matter of the dragon, if You're not tired of it by this time."

"Yes, come in, Boy," said the Saint, kindly. "Another tale of misery and wrong, I fear me."

"Is it a kind parent, then, of whom the tyrant has bereft you? Or some tender sister or brother? Well, it shall soon be avenged."

"Nothing of the sort," said the Boy. "There's a misunderstanding somewhere, and I want to put it right. The fact is, this is a good dragon."

"Exactly," said St George, smiling pleasantly, "I quite understand. A good dragon. Believe me, I do not in the least regret that he is an adversary worthy of my steel, and no feeble specimen of his noxious tribe."

"But He's not a noxious tribe," cried the Boy, distressed. "Oh dear, oh dear, how stupid men are when they get an idea into their heads! I tell you He's a good dragon, and a friend of mine, and tells me the most beautiful stories you ever heard, all about old times and when he was little. And He's been so kind to mother, and mother would do anything for him. And father likes him too, though father doesn't hold with art and poetry much, and always falls asleep when the dragon starts talking about style. But the fact is, nobody can help liking him once they know him. He's so engaging and so trustful, and as simple as a child!"

"Sit down, and draw your chair up," said St George. "I like a fellow who sticks up for his friends, and I'm sure the dragon has his good points, if He's got a friend like you. But That's not the question. All this evening I've been listening, with grief and unspeakable anguish, to tales of murder, theft, and wrong; rather too highly colored, perhaps, not always quite convincing, but forming in the main a most serious roll of crime. History teaches us that the greatest rascals often possess all the domestic virtues; and I fear that your cultivated friend, in spite of the qualities which have won (and rightly) your regard, has got to be speedily exterminated."

"Oh, you've been taking in all the yarns those fellows have been telling you," said the Boy, impatiently. "Why, our villagers are the biggest storytellers in all the country round. It's a known fact. You're a stranger in these parts, or else You'd have heard it already. All they want is a fight. They're the most awful beggars for getting up fights— It's meat and drink to them. Dogs, bulls, dragons—anything so long as It's a fight.

Why, they've got a poor innocent badger in the stable behind here, at this moment. They were going to have some fun with him today, but they're saving him up now till your little affair's over. And I've no doubt they've been telling you what a hero you were, and how you were bound to win, in the cause of right and justice, and so on; but let me tell you, I came down the street just now, and they were betting six to four on the dragon freely!"

"Six to four on the dragon!" murmured St George, sadly, resting his cheek on his hand. "This is an evil world, and sometimes I begin to think that all the wickedness in it is not entirely bottled up inside the dragons. And yet—may not this wily beast have misled you as to his real character, in order that your good report of him may serve as a cloak for his evil deeds? Nay, may there not be, at this very moment, some hapless Princess immured within yonder gloomy cavern?"

The moment he had spoken, St George was sorry for what he had said, the Boy looked so genuinely distressed.

"I assure you, St George," he said earnestly, "there's nothing of the sort in the cave at all. The dragon's a real gentleman, every inch of him, and I may say that no one would be more shocked and grieved than he would, at hearing you talk in that—that loose way about matters on which he has very strong views!"

"Well, perhaps I've been over-credulous," said St George. "Perhaps I've misjudged the animal. But what are we to do? Here are the dragon and I, almost face to face, each supposed to be thirsting for each other's blood. I don't see any way out of it, exactly. What do you suggest? Can't you arrange things, somehow?"

"That's just what the dragon said," replied the Boy, rather nettled. "Really, the way you two seem to leave everything to me—I suppose you couldn't be persuaded to go away quietly, could you?"

"Impossible, I fear," said the Saint. "Quite against the rules. You know that as well as I do."
"Well, then, look here," said the Boy, "It's early yet—would you mind strolling up with me and seeing the dragon and talking it over? It's not far, and any friend of mine will be most welcome."

"Well, It's irregular," said St George, rising, "but really it seems about the most sensible thing to do. You're taking a lot of trouble on your friend's account," he added, good- naturedly, as they passed out through the door together. "But cheer up! Perhaps there won't have to be any fight after all."

"Oh, but I hope there will, though!" replied the little fellow, wistfully. "I've brought a friend to see you, dragon," said the Boy, rather loud.

The dragon woke up with a start. "I was just-er-thinking about things," he said in his simple way. "Very pleased to make your acquaintance, sir. Charming weather we're having!"

"This is St George," said the Boy, shortly. "St George, let me introduce you to the dragon. We've come up to talk things over quietly, dragon, and now for goodness" sake do let us have a little straight common-sense, and come to some practical business-like arrangement, for I'm sick of views and theories of life and personal tendencies, and all that sort of thing. I may perhaps add that my mother's sitting up."

"So glad to meet you, St George," began the dragon, rather nervously, "because you've been a great traveler, I hear, and I've always been rather stay-at-home. But I can show you many antiquities, many interesting features of our countryside, if You're stopping here any time—"

"I think," said St George, in his frank, pleasant way, "that we'd really better take the advice of our young friend here, and try to come to some understanding, on a business footing, about this little affair of ours. Now don't you think that after all the simplest plan would be just to fight it out, according to the rules, and let the best man win? They're betting on you, I may tell you, down in the village, but I don't mind that!"

"Oh, yes, do, dragon," said the Boy, delightedly; "it'll save such a lot of bother!"

"My young friend, you shut up," said the dragon, severely. "Believe me, St George," he went on, "there's nobody in the world I'd sooner oblige than you and this young gentleman here. But the whole thing's nonsense, and conventionality, and popular thick-headedness. There's absolutely nothing to fight about, from beginning to end. And anyhow I'm not going to, so that settles it!"

"But supposing I make you?" said St George, rather nettled. "You can't," said the dragon, triumphantly. "I should only go into my cave and retire for a time down the hole I came up. You'd soon get heartily sick of sitting outside and waiting for me to come out and fight you. And as soon as You'd really gone away, why, I'd come up again gaily, for I tell you frankly, I like this place, and I'm going to stay here!"

St George gazed for a while on the fair landscape around them. "But this would be a beautiful place for a fight," he began again persuasively. "These great bare rolling Downs for the arena, —and me in my golden armor showing up against your big blue scaly coils! Think what a picture it would make!"

"Now You're trying to get at me through my artistic sensibilities," said the dragon. "But it won't work. Not but what it would make a very pretty picture, as you say," he added, wavering a little.

"We seem to be getting rather nearer to business," put in the Boy. "You must see, dragon, that there's got to be a fight of some sort, 'cos you can't want to have to go down that dirty old hole again and stop there till goodness knows when."

"It might be arranged," said St George, thoughtfully. "I must spear you somewhere, of course, but I'm not bound to hurt you very much. There's such a lot of you that there must be a few spare places somewhere. Here, for instance, just behind your foreleg. It couldn't hurt you much, just here!"

"Now You're tickling, George," said the dragon, coyly. "No, that place won't do at all. Even if it didn't hurt,—and I'm sure it would, awfully,—it would make me laugh, and that would spoil everything."

"Let's try somewhere else, then," said St George, patiently. "Under your neck, for instance, —all these folds of thick skin, —if I speared you here You'd never even know I'd done it!"

"Yes, but are you sure you can hit off the right place?" asked the dragon, anxiously.

"Of course I am," said St George, with confidence. "You leave that to me!"

## Wrap-Up: Storytelling in Context

The historical context reminds us that Grahame was writing at the turn of the twentieth century, gently poking fun at heroic conventions.

Understanding this backdrop allows us to highlight the story's irony without losing its charm. The narrative and character arcs give shape to performance: the Shepherd's fear, the Boy's steady confidence, the Dragon's reluctant indolence, and St. George's noble formality all create distinct beats for the teller to follow.

Actor and voice actor techniques invite us to layer tone, pacing, and vocal contrast so that listeners hear not only a fable but a living conversation between unlikely friends. Expanding into staging reminds us that this is not only a story to be read, but one that can be embodied—on a bare stage, in a classroom, or around a fireside. The simplicity of its characters and settings makes it adaptable: a solo performer can hold the tale with voice and gesture, or a small cast can bring out its humor through playful interaction.

Together, these perspectives remind us that *The Reluctant Dragon* is less about slaying monsters than about reframing them. It is a story where performance—whether spoken, staged, or shared across a page—becomes part of the message: that stories themselves can tame fear, overturn expectation, and open space for gentler truths.

Whether told aloud, dramatized with friends, or read quietly on the page, Grahame's fable continues to whisper that imagination is stronger than violence, and that even dragons may choose poetry over battle.

Consider how you might stage or voice this story in your own context. Every retelling reimagines the legend.

In the end, performance becomes both art and argument — showing that even in an age of spectacle, quiet stories still hold power.

# Epilogue

Kenneth Grahame gave us a dragon who would rather write poetry than fight, a boy who trusted reason over fear, and a knight willing to bend the rules. In their meeting, he created a fable not of conquest but of imagination— a gentle rebellion against the heroic ideals of his age. First appearing in *Dream Days* (1898), *The Reluctant Dragon* asks whether true strength lies in the sword or in understanding: a story where courage is measured by compassion, and even tradition learns to yield to kindness.

For readers and performers alike, this fable offers a mirror. It invites us to question which roles we have inherited and which we might choose to outgrow. The humor, so light on the surface, conceals a quiet radicalism— suggesting that peace and imagination are the truest forms of courage.

Sharing this story today is itself an act of reimagining.

It reminds us that stories are not monuments to the past—they move and breathe, changing shape each time a new voice brings them to life. Every reading, every performance, becomes a renewal of imagination; a reminder that creativity and compassion are never out of date.

The boy, the dragon, and the knight still find one another wherever people choose curiosity over certainty, conversation over conflict, playfulness over pride.

They meet in classrooms and on stages, around microphones and kitchen tables—anywhere a story dares to be retold.

And in that shared moment, the legend continues—not as a tale of battle won, but as living proof that empathy outlasts fear, and that the quiet courage to listen remains the most transformative act of all.

# Bonus Material

## ***Dream Days: Kenneth Grahame's World of Imagination and Rebellion***

To understand *The Reluctant Dragon*, one must step into *Dream Days* (1898), the collection where it first appeared. These stories, written as much for adults as for children, celebrate imagination as quiet defiance—a gentle antidote to the rigid respectability of late Victorian life.

### Childhood and the Country of Dreams

Kenneth Grahame's early life was shaped by both loss and landscape. Born in Edinburgh in 1859, he lost his mother at five, and his father—unable to care for the children—sent them to live with their grandmother in the Berkshire countryside. The meadows and riverbanks of Cookham Dean became his emotional homeland and later his literary terrain. There, he discovered the sacredness of small things: a dragonfly, a stream, a shifting play of light through trees.

These impressions became the heart of *The Golden Age* (1895) and *Dream Days* (1898), where childhood is not something to be escaped but remembered as a state of deeper truth. Grahame's voice, nostalgic yet unsentimental, honors the inner life of the child and the power of wonder to reveal meaning.

### A Civil Servant with a Rebel's Imagination

By day, Grahame served as a senior official at the Bank of England; by night, he wrote of rivers, woods, and mischief. His imagination roamed far beyond the confines of London's order and hierarchy. In *Dream Days*, he quietly rejected moral instruction and glorified duty, choosing instead to elevate play, curiosity, and empathy. His prose suggests that fantasy is not escape but insight—an alternate way of knowing the world.

## The Reluctant Dragon and the Art of Inversion

Within this collection, *The Reluctant Dragon* stands apart. Its humor and irony transform a familiar legend into a meditation on creativity and courage. By letting the dragon speak—and speak with wit and grace—Grahame reversed centuries of convention. The so-called monster becomes poet and philosopher, while the traditional hero learns mercy. It is both a fable and a commentary on storytelling itself: who gets to tell the tale, and how the telling shapes the truth.

## Excerpt from the Preface to *Dream Days*

> "It was in those days that the little things of life, the trifles light as air, acquired for us a strange significance and value. A bird's note, the smell of a flower, a glimpse of a far horizon, would be to us events of moment; full of mysterious meaning, hinting of things beyond our ken."

This passage captures Grahame's creative creed—that imagination can uncover truths reason cannot.

## Legacy and Later Echoes

*Dream Days* laid the groundwork for *The Wind in the Willows* (1908), expanding Grahame's vision of friendship, nature, and the quiet joys of ordinary life. Mole, Rat, and Badger inherit the gentleness and humor first seen in the Boy and the Dragon.

Over the next century, *The Reluctant Dragon* never vanished. Adapted for stage and screen—most famously in Disney's 1941 feature—it has endured as a story that welcomes reinterpretation. Each new version rediscovers its civility, its wit, and its soft-spoken courage.

**Why It Still Speaks**

In an age that prizes speed, certainty, and spectacle, Grahame's refusal to rush or roar feels quietly revolutionary. His world invites readers to pause, listen, and rediscover the grace of being human. Through *Dream Days*, he left us a map back to gentleness—a landscape where imagination and empathy still meet, and even the fiercest dragons can be coaxed into conversation.

# More from Lemery House Press

Discover more stories of reflection, resilience, and imagination.
in the True Voice Shorts series.

Available in enhanced audio and literary editions at:
www.LemeryHousePress.com

**Listen. Read. Remember.**

www.ingramcontent.com/pod-product-compliance
Lightning Source LLC
Chambersburg PA
CBHW050441200726
48295CB00024B/934

* 9 7 8 1 9 5 7 7 6 3 4 1 5 *